D0298218

Marshall Morgan and Scott
Marshall Pickering
3 Beggarwood Lane, Basingstoke, Hants. RG23 7LP
Reprinted 1986

Text and illustrations © Nick Butterworth and Mick Inkpen 1986

First published by Marshall Morgan & Scott in 1986

British Library Cataloguing in Publication Data
Butterworth, Nick
The two sons.
1. Two sons (Parable)-Juvenile literature
2. Bible stories, English-N.T.
I. Title II. Inkpen, Mick
226'.809505   BT378.T/
ISBN 0-551-01280-3

Printed in Great Britain by
W.S. Cowell Limited, Ipswich

The Two Sons

Nick Butterworth and Mick Inkpen

MARSHALL MORGAN & SCOTT

Here is a man.
He grows apples in an orchard.

The apples are red and rosy.
It is time for them to be picked.

At home the man has two sons.

'I want you to help me to pick
the apples' says the man to
his first son.
'No,' says the first son.
'I'm busy.'

But after a while he is sorry
for what he said.
He picks up a basket and goes
to the orchard.

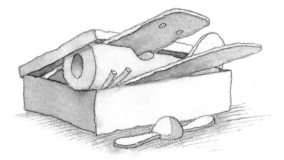

The man finds his second son.
'I want you to help me pick
the apples too,' he says.

'Yes,' says the second son.
'I will come as soon as I have
put on my boots.'

Back in the orchard the first son is busy picking apples. Look, he has already filled one basket.

'Well done son,' says the man.
'Here is another basket.
We'll have this done in no time.'

They work together until all
the apples have been picked.
But there is no sign of the
second son.
He has forgotten his promise.

Who do you think pleased his father?
The first son or the second son?

Jesus says,
'What we do is
more important
than what
we say.'